I0393396

The Victorious Letter V

Coloring Book

By Peggy Louise Parrish
C. 2017

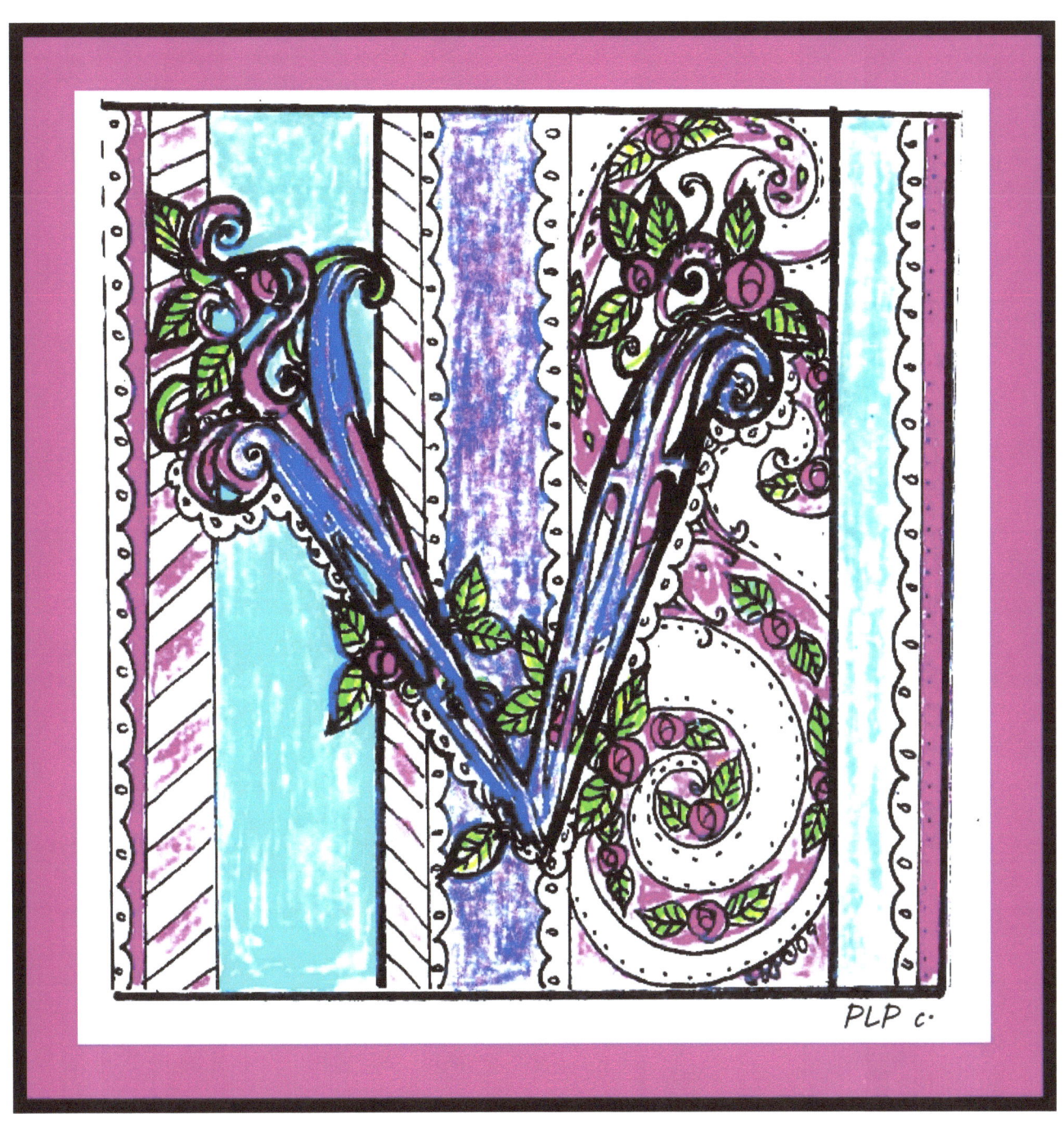

Welcome to the Victorious Letter V Adventure!

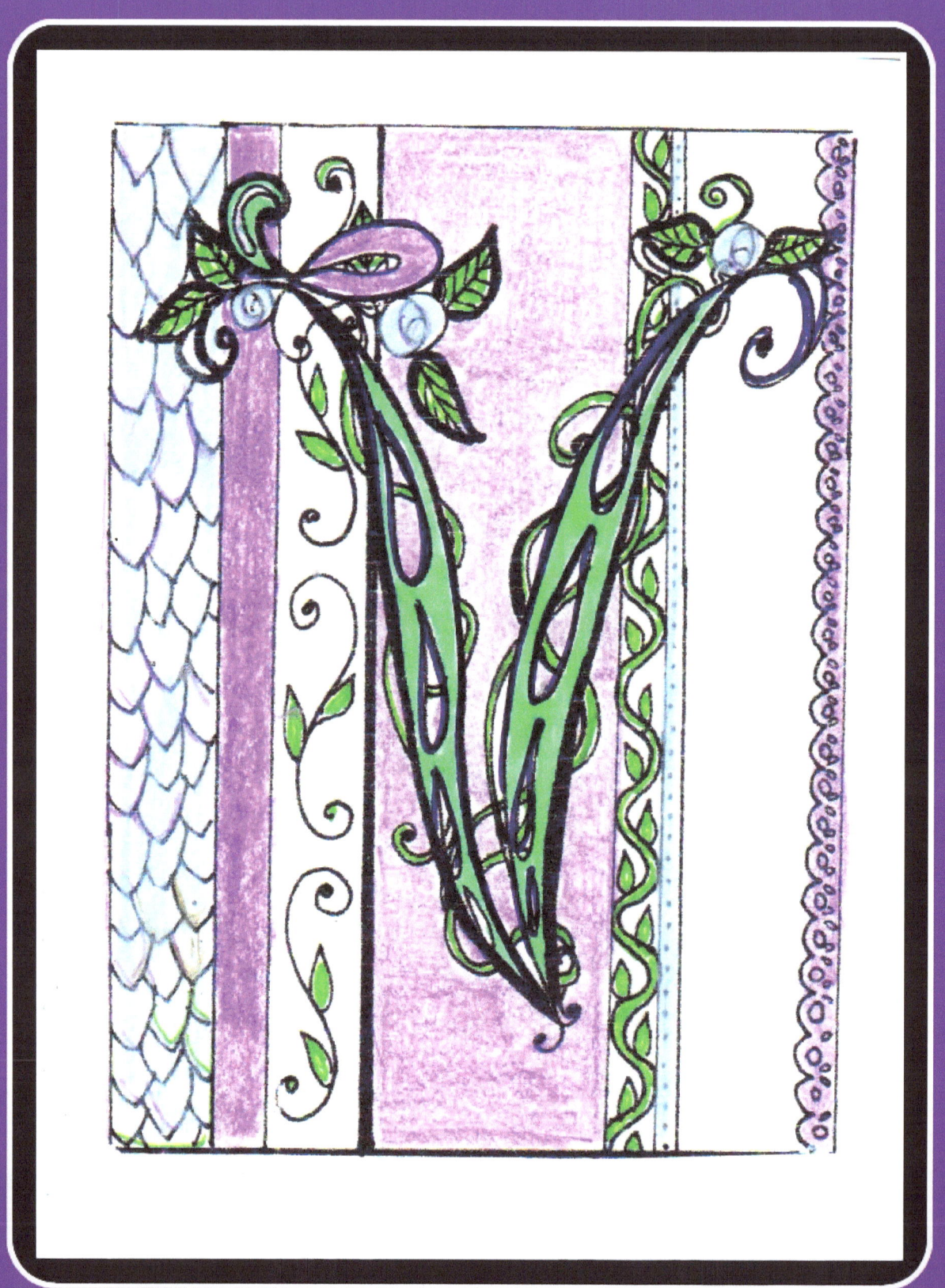

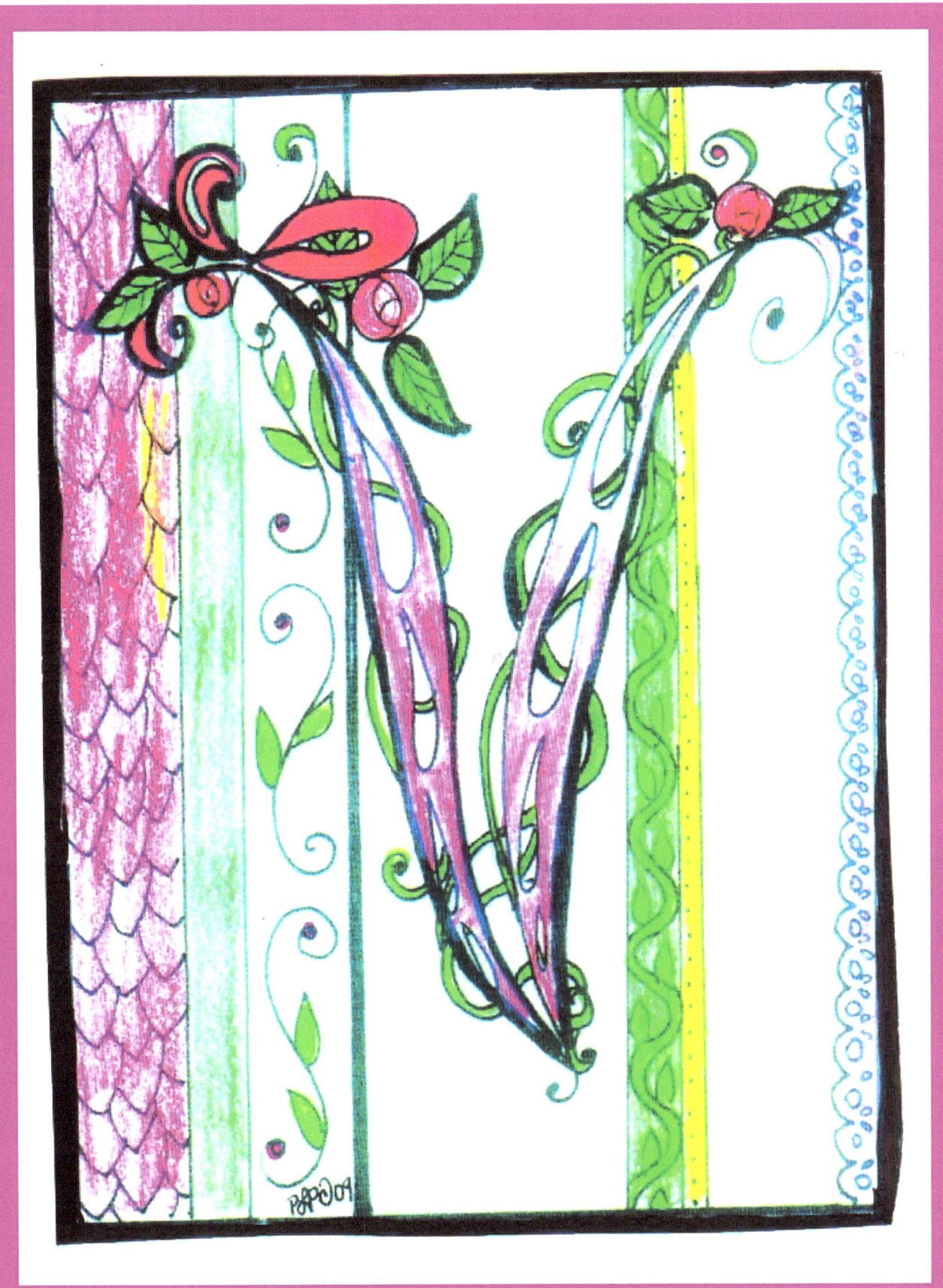

Welcome to the Victorious Letter V collection. There are 20 designs of the Letter V that were originated by artist Peggy Louise Parrish. Leave her initials at the bottom of the letters please. You may make a few"in house" copies of the particular V letters you like the most to color in different ways. You may make copies of your work for yourself or a gift. No selling of these letters is allowed.

The preferred medium for these pages is usually quality colored pencils. If you want to try gel pens, markers, paints or watercolor pencils be sure to place a scrap paper under your work.

Perhaps your first or last name begins with the letter V. Or maybe you have a friend with letter V or a word that needs a drop cap letter V colored your style. Hopefully you will have some fun with these pages. ENJOY! Color till your heart's content.

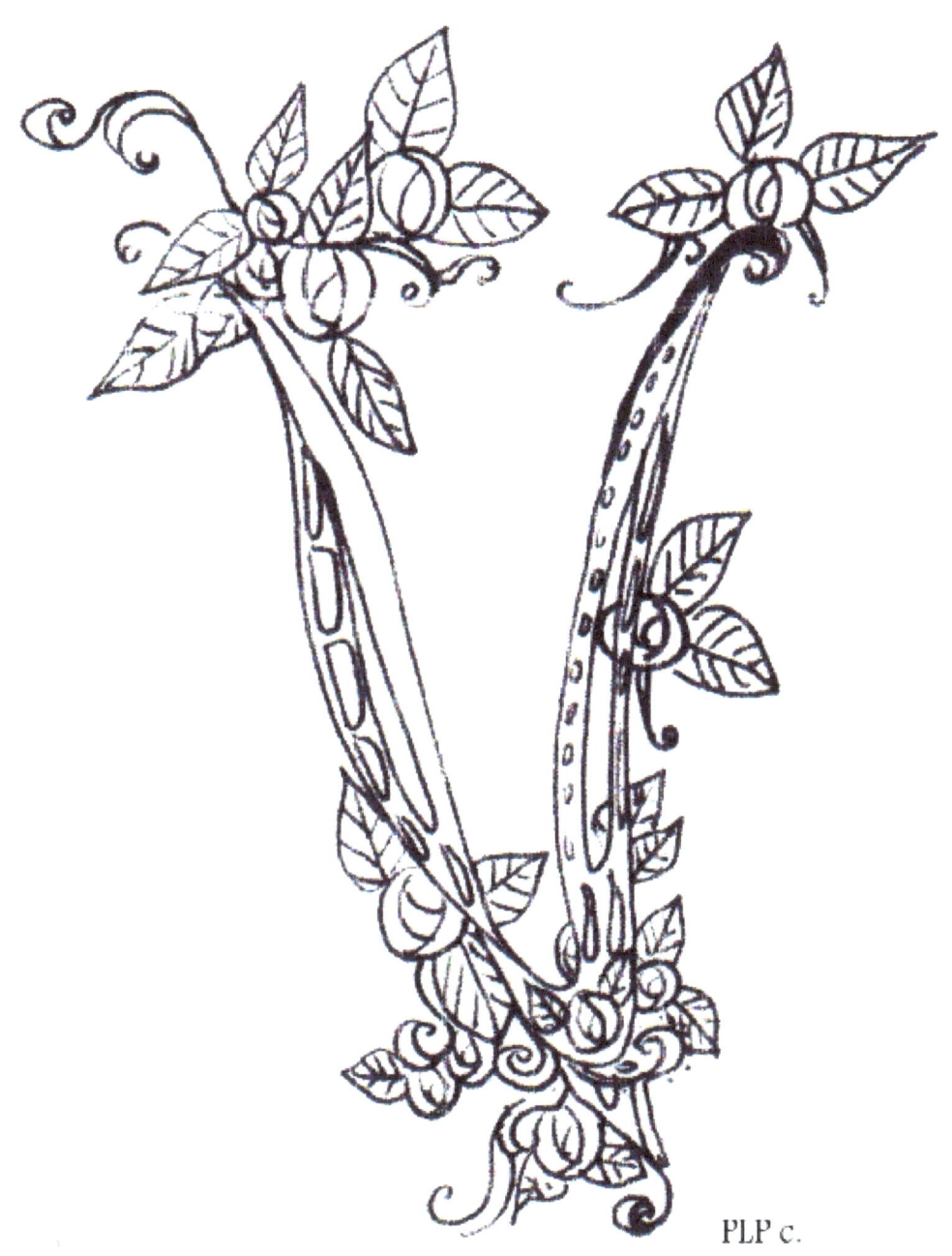

PLP c.

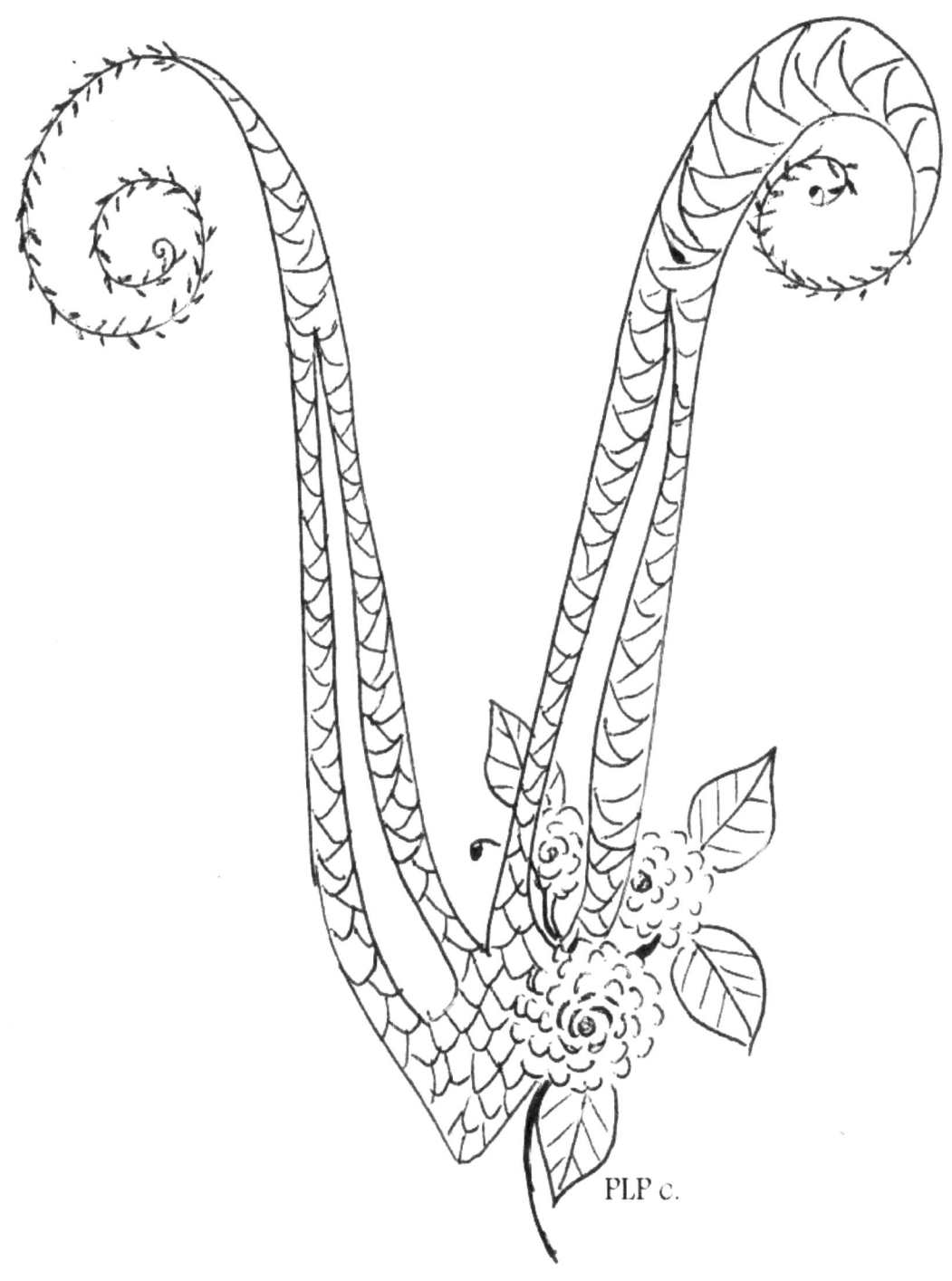

PLP c.

13

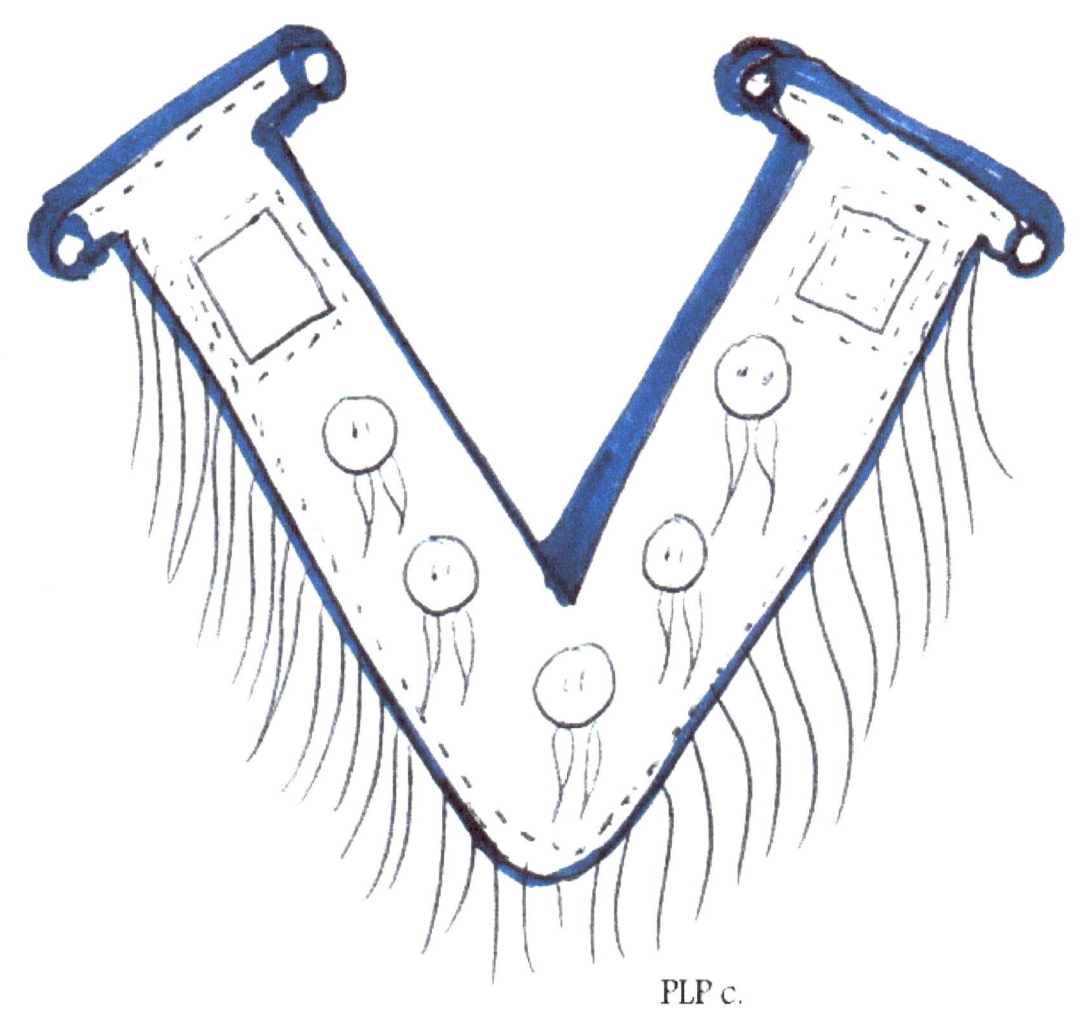

PLP c.

15

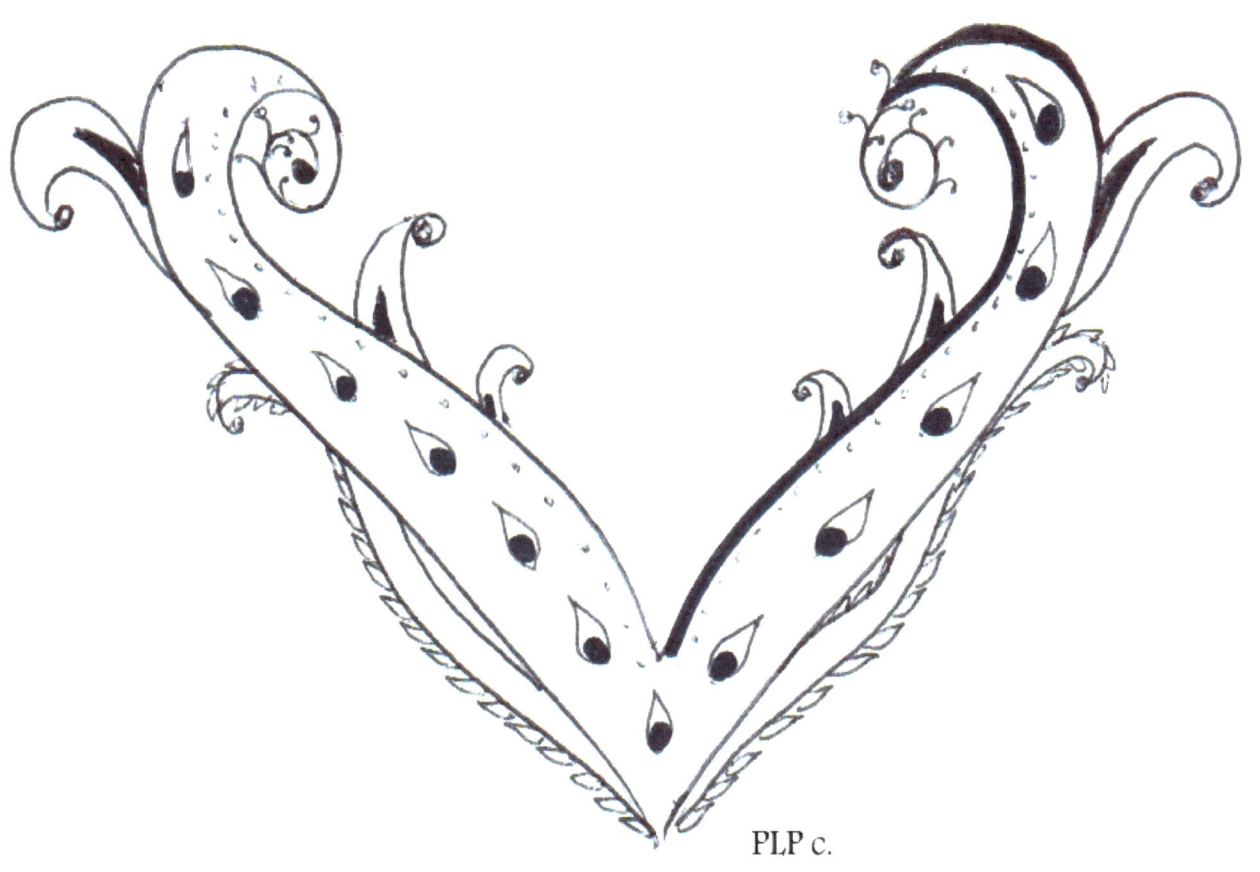

PLP c.

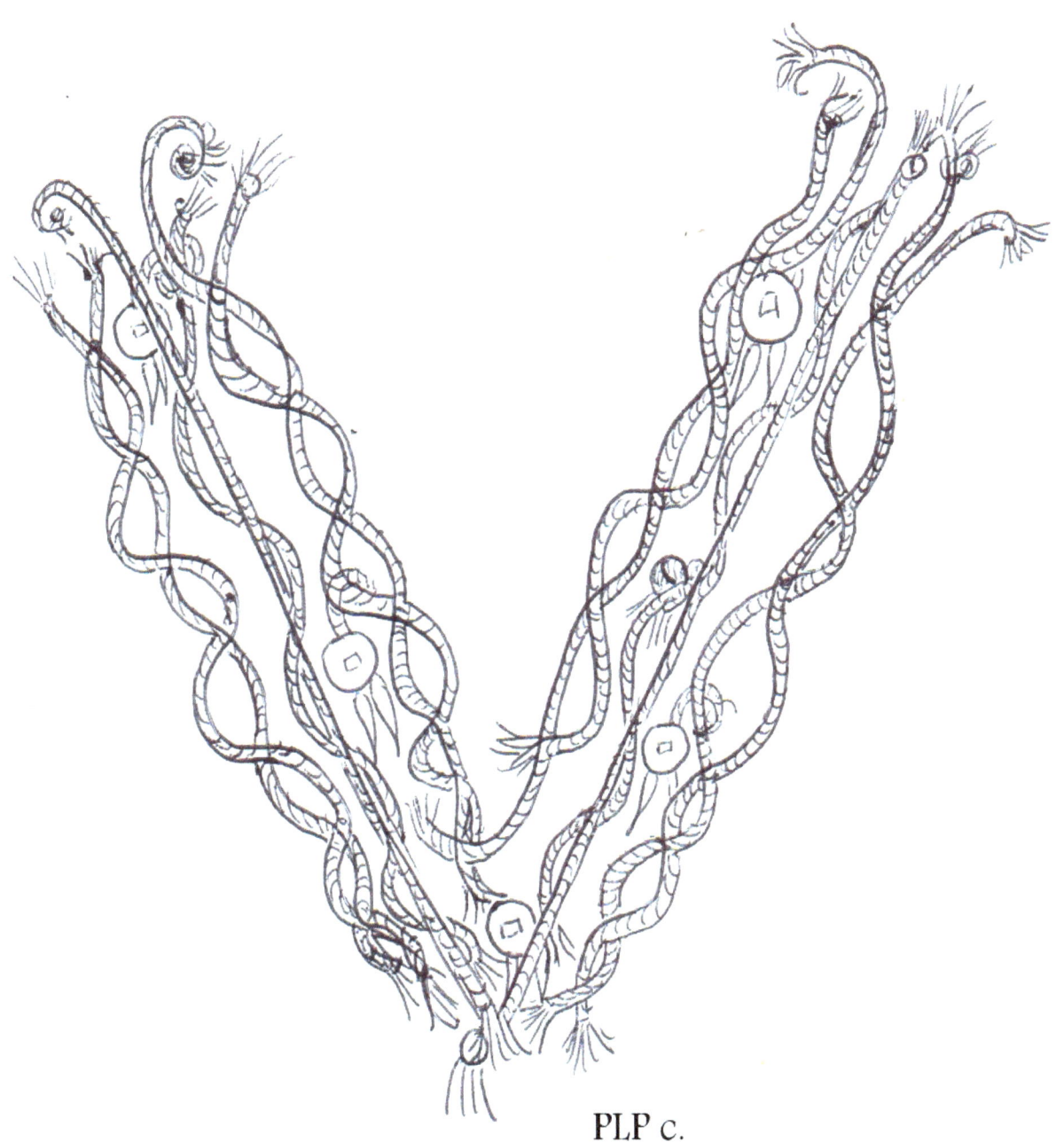

PLP c.

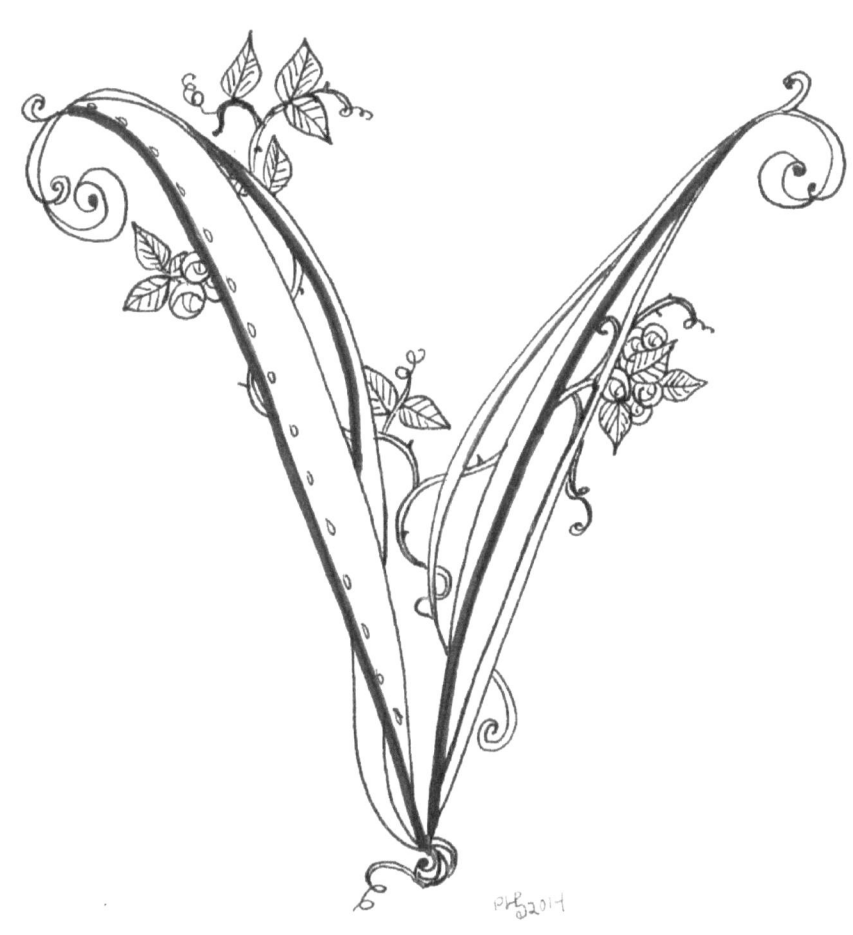

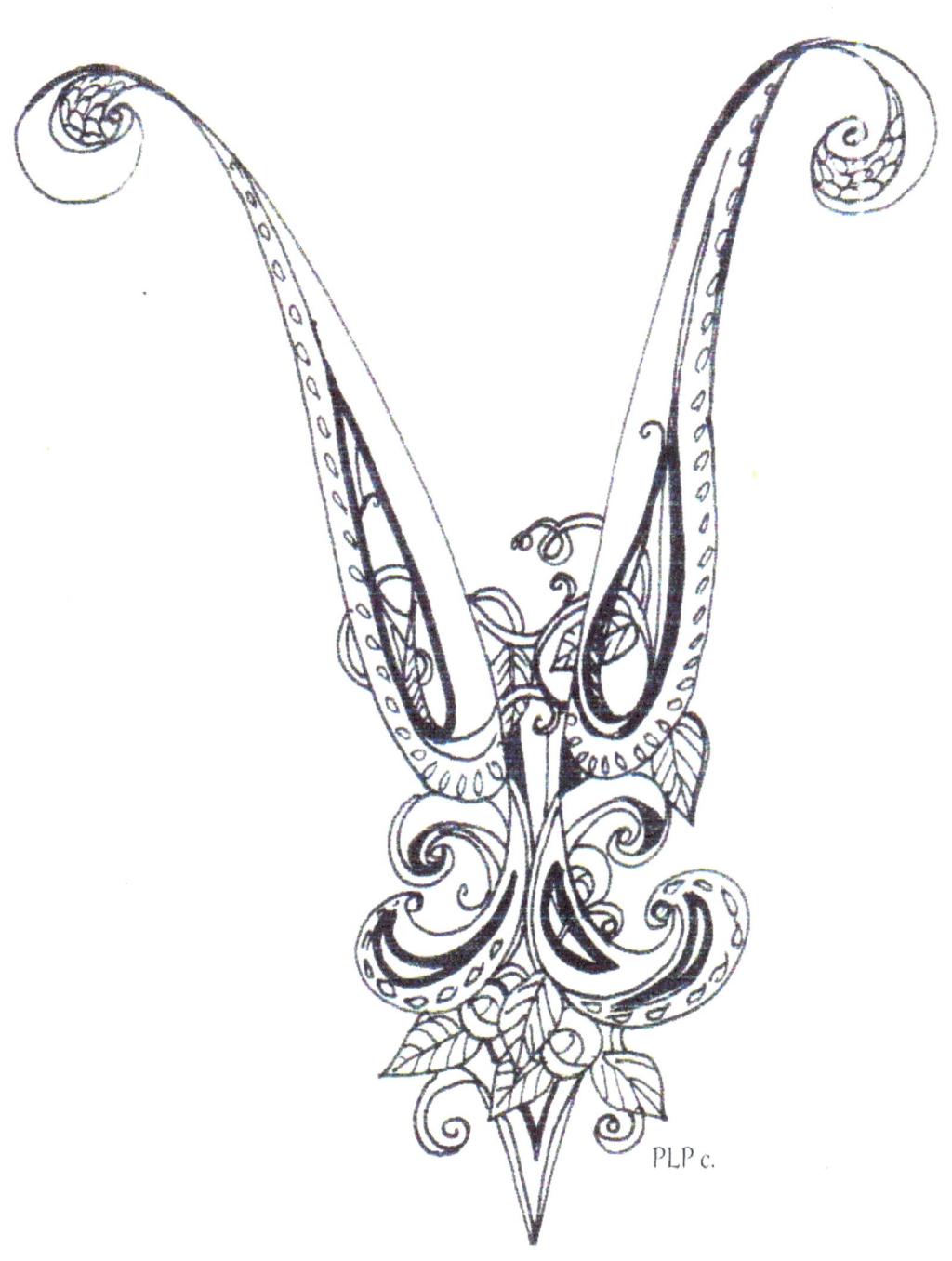

PLP c.

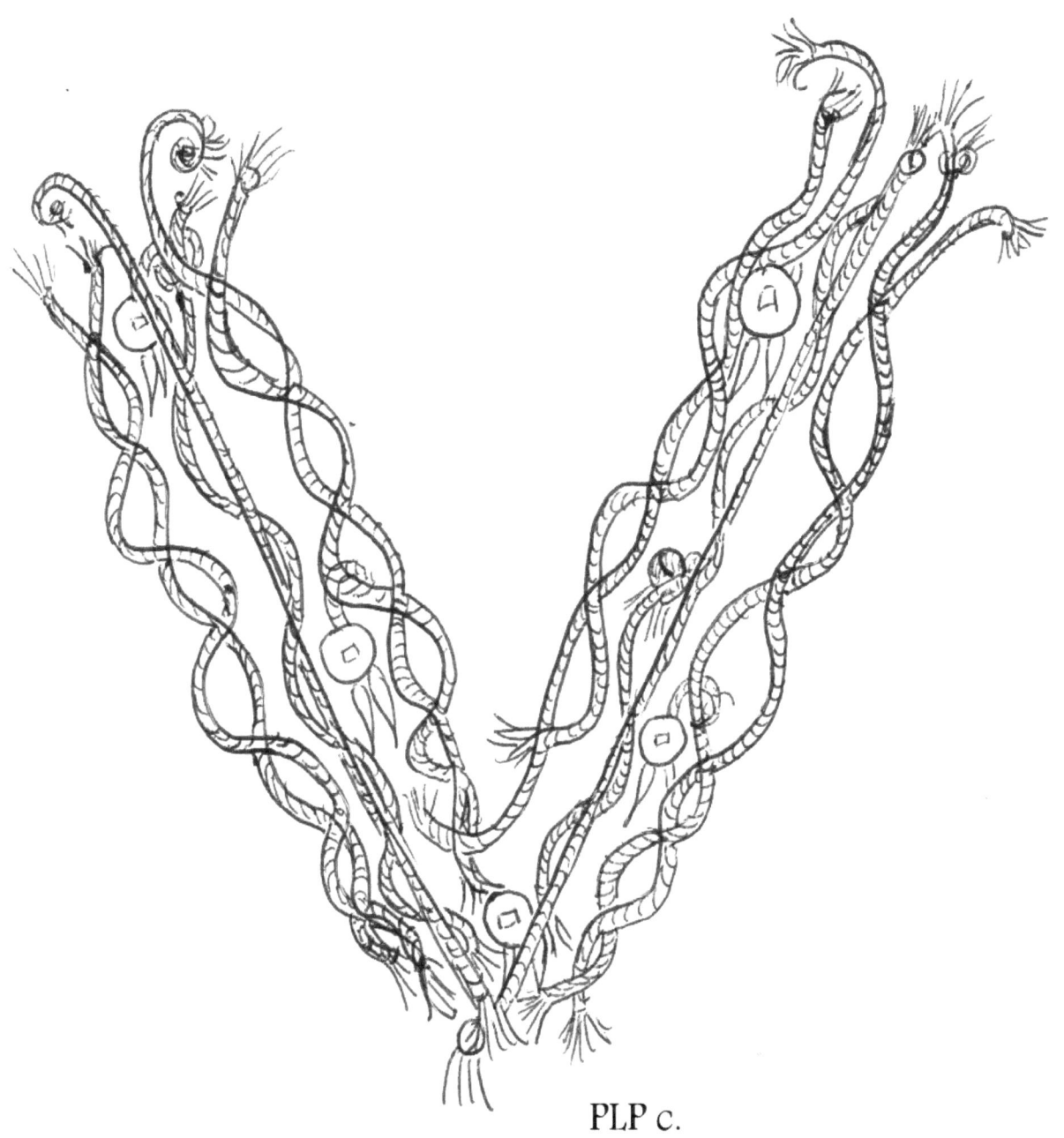

PLP c.

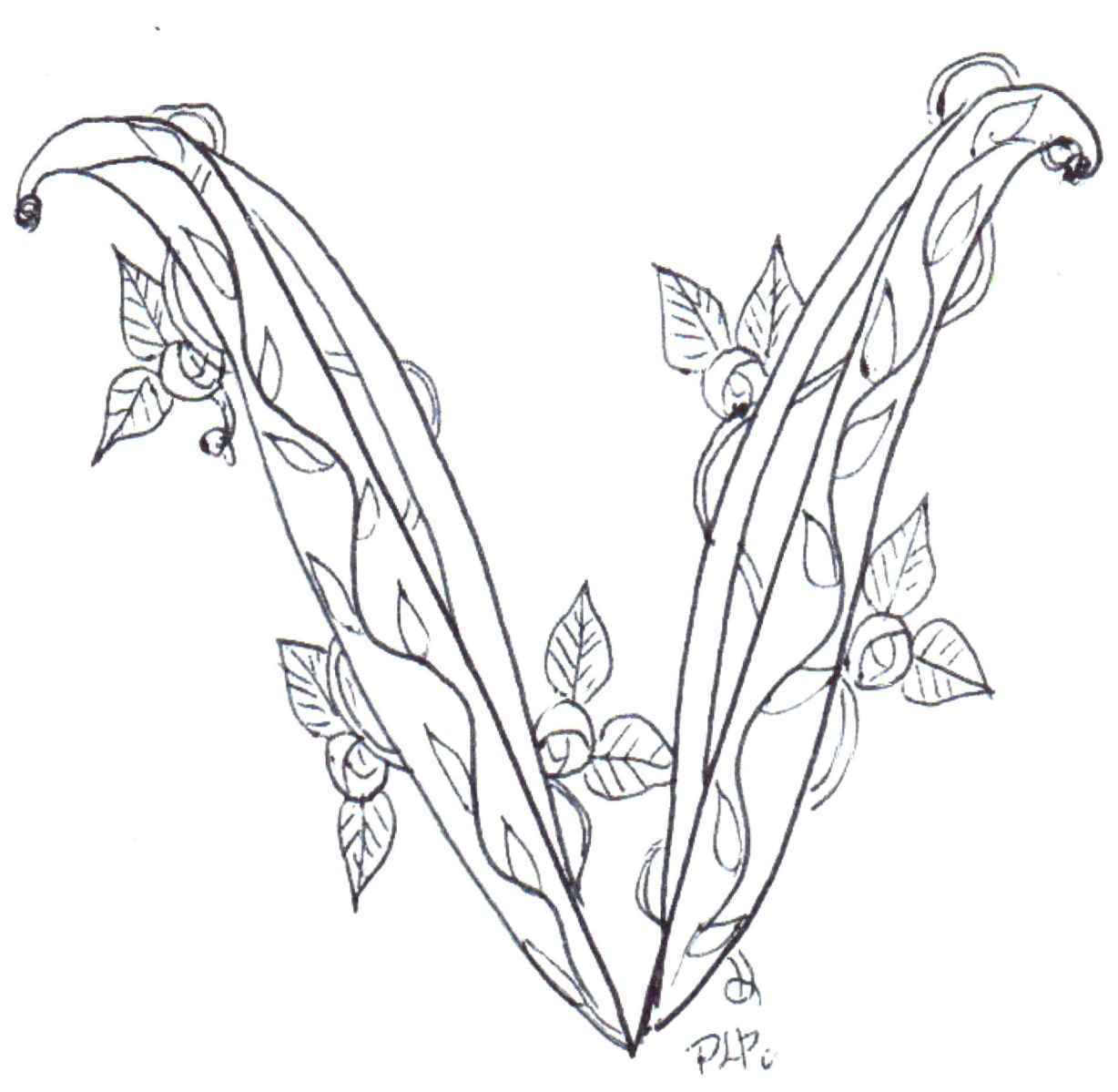

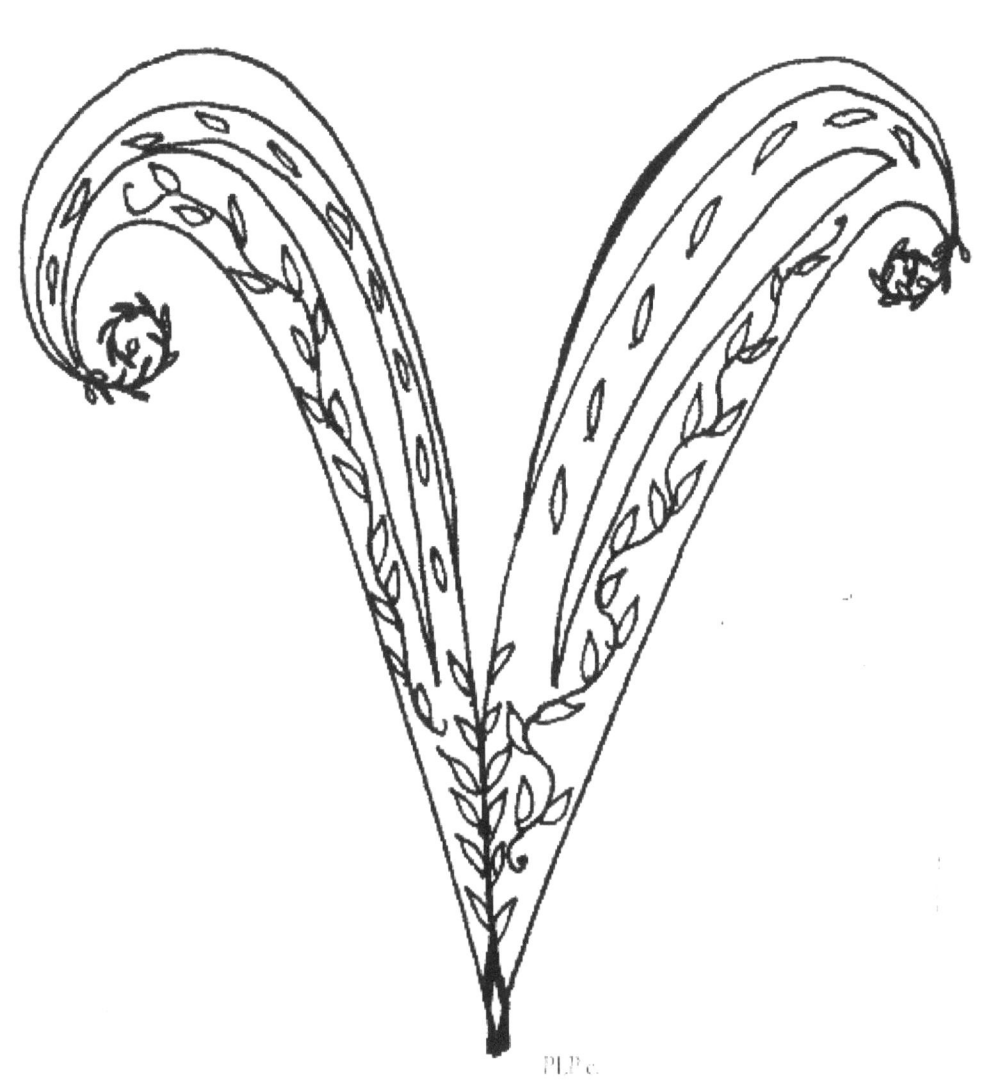

PLP c.

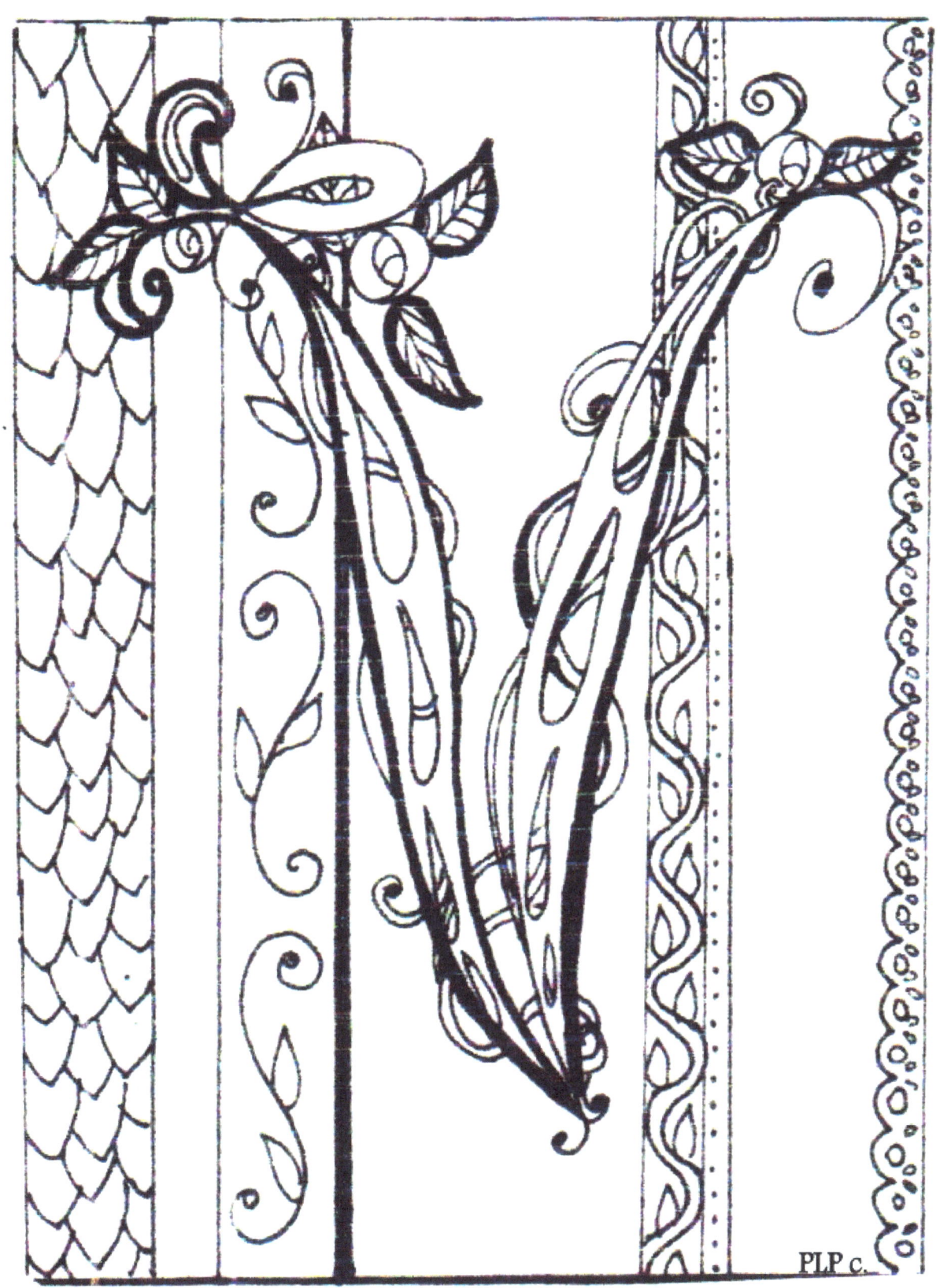

PLP c.

31

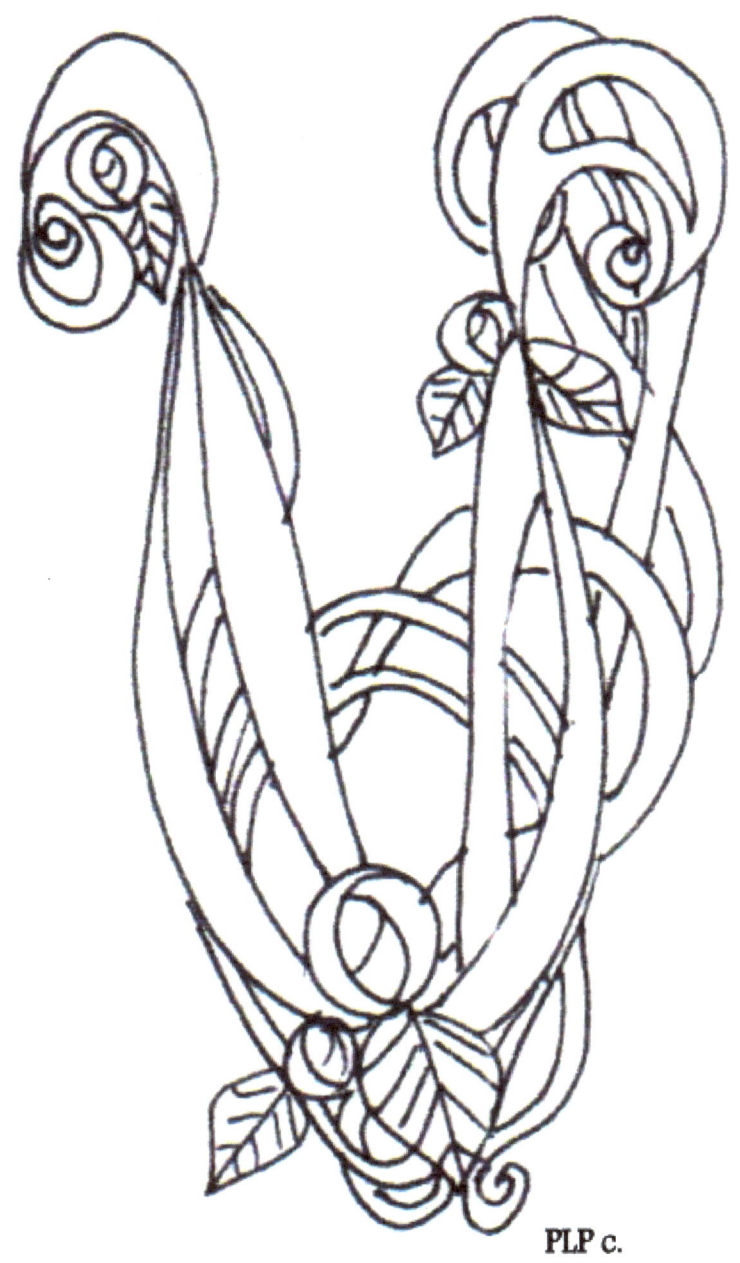

PLP c.

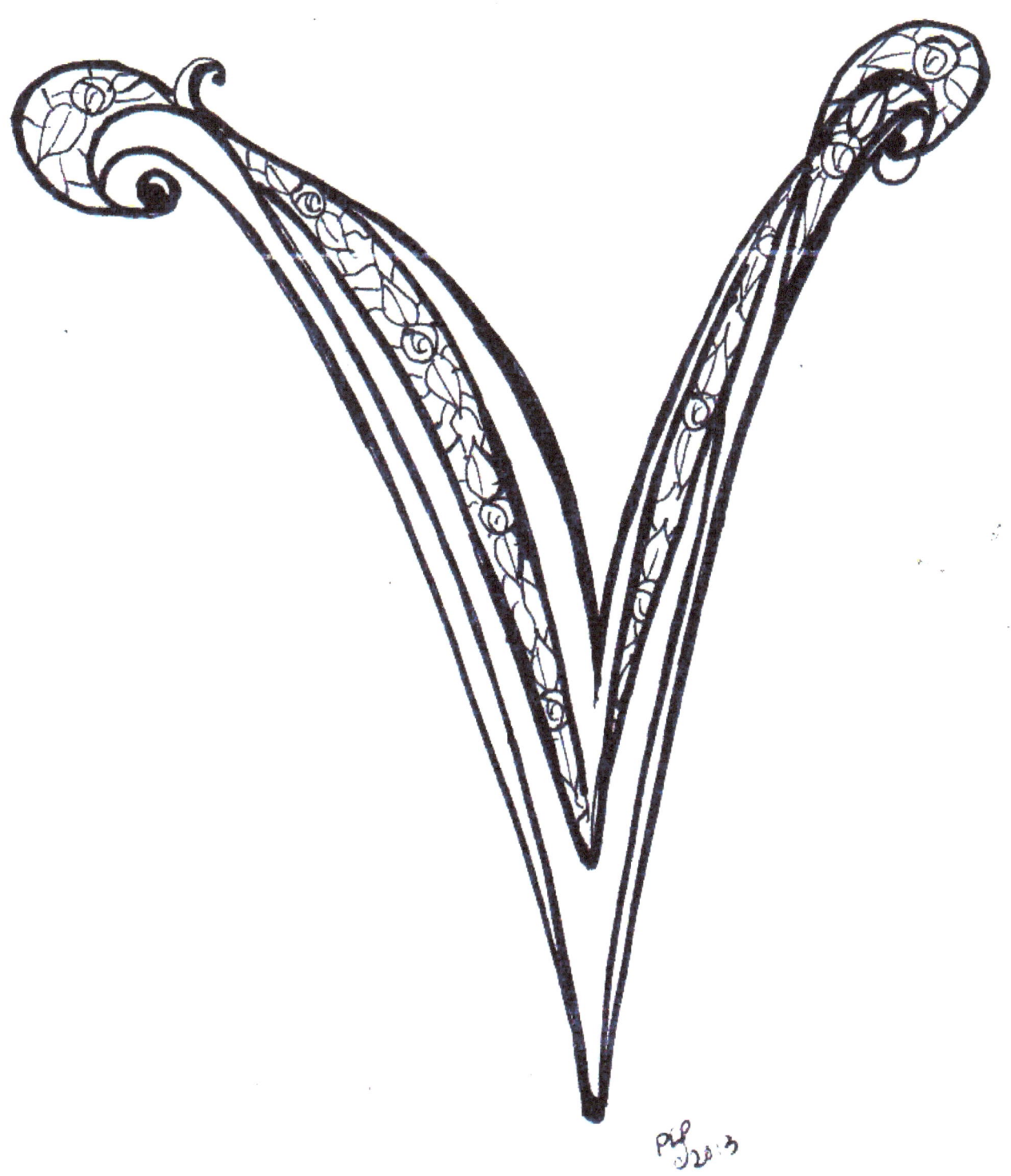

PL 2013

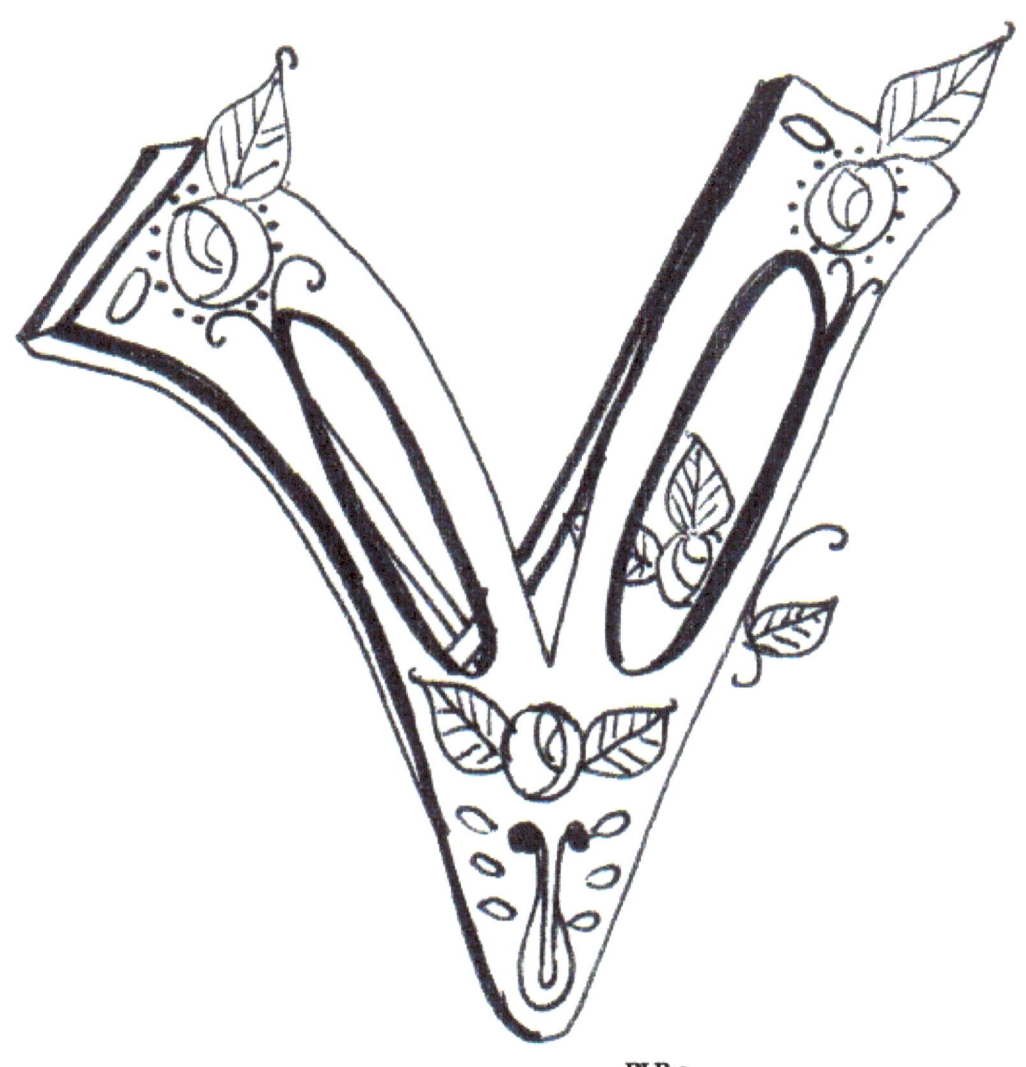

PLP c.

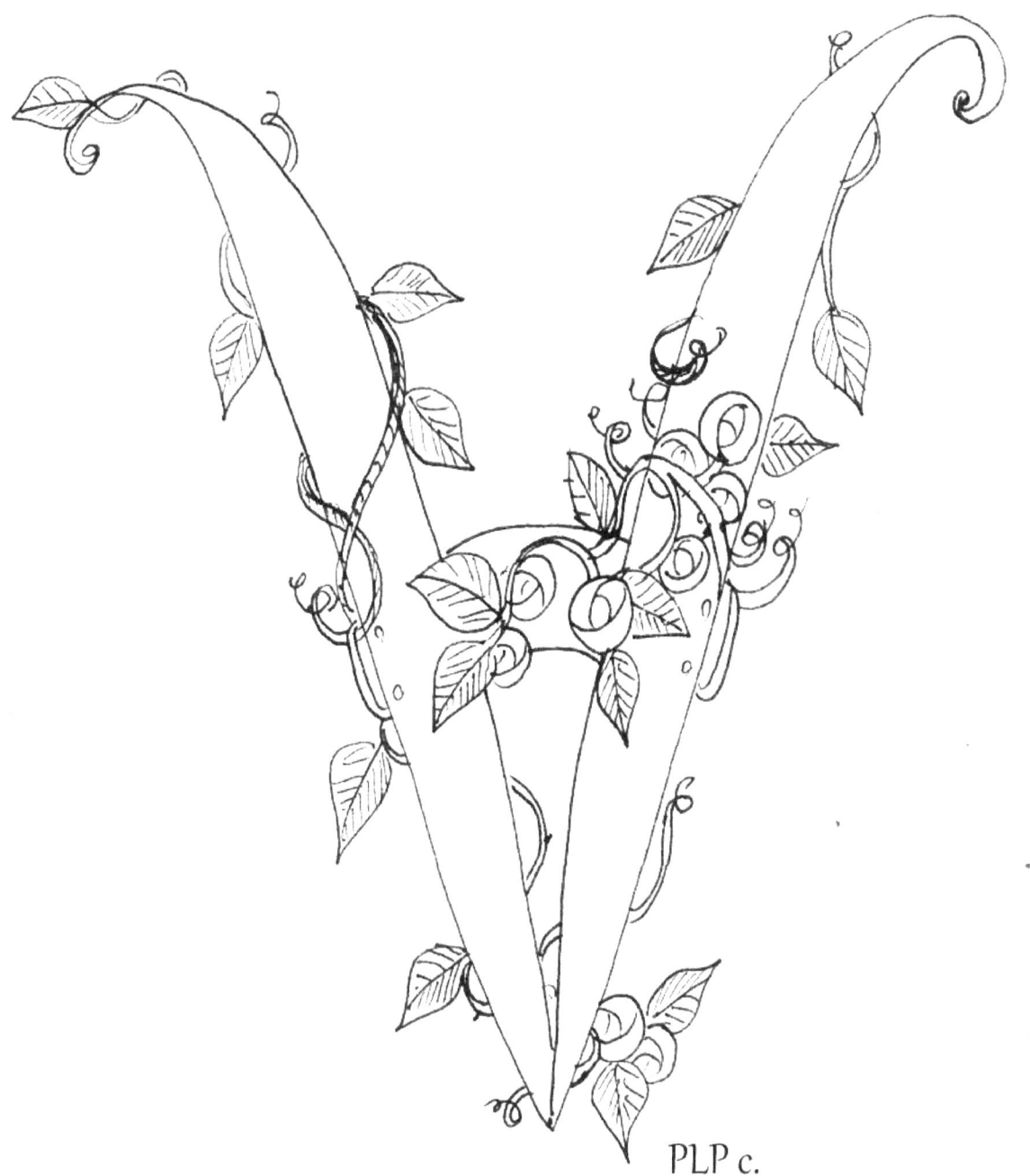

PLP c.

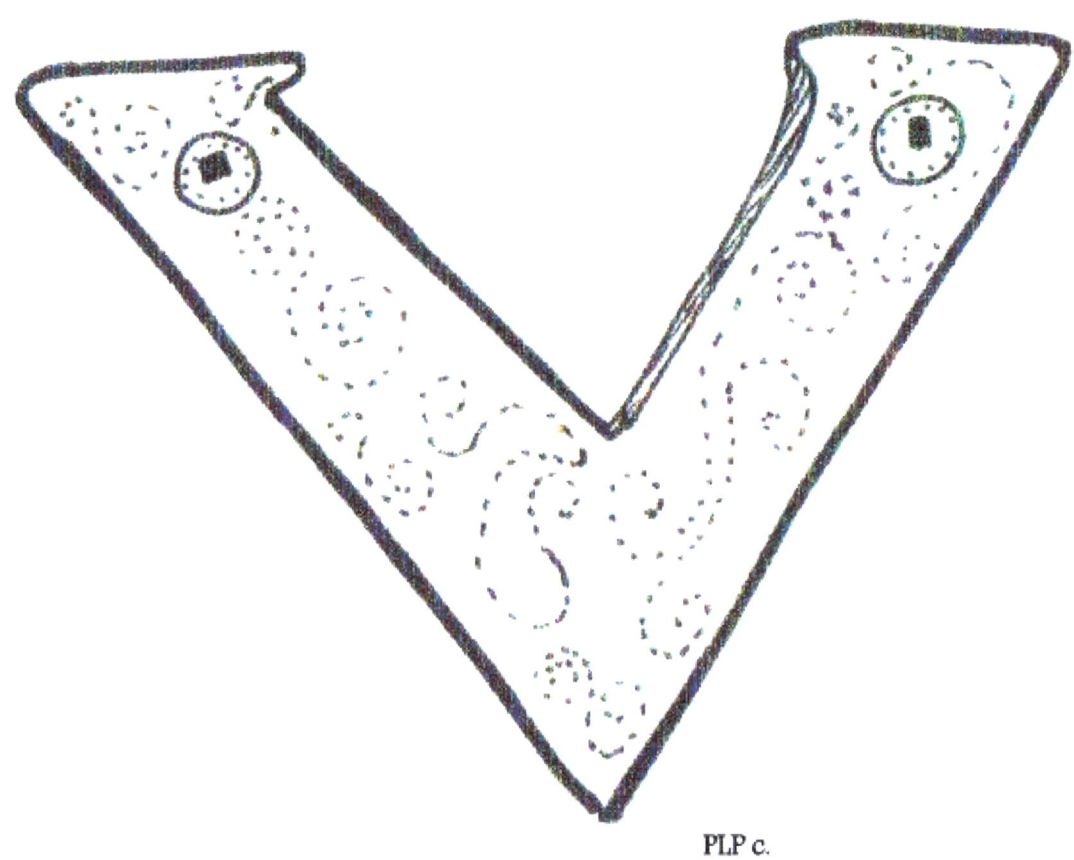

PLP c.

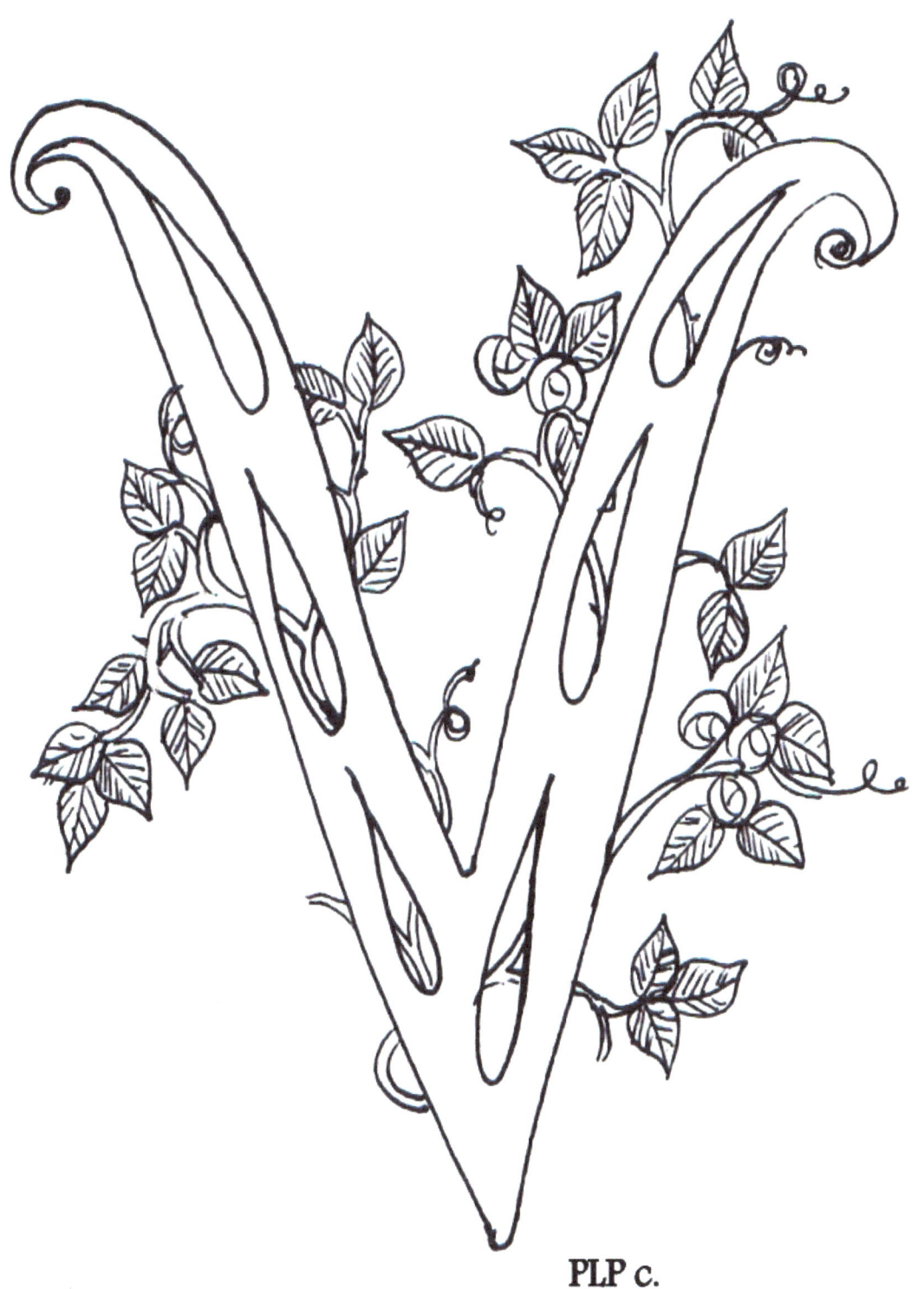

PLP c.

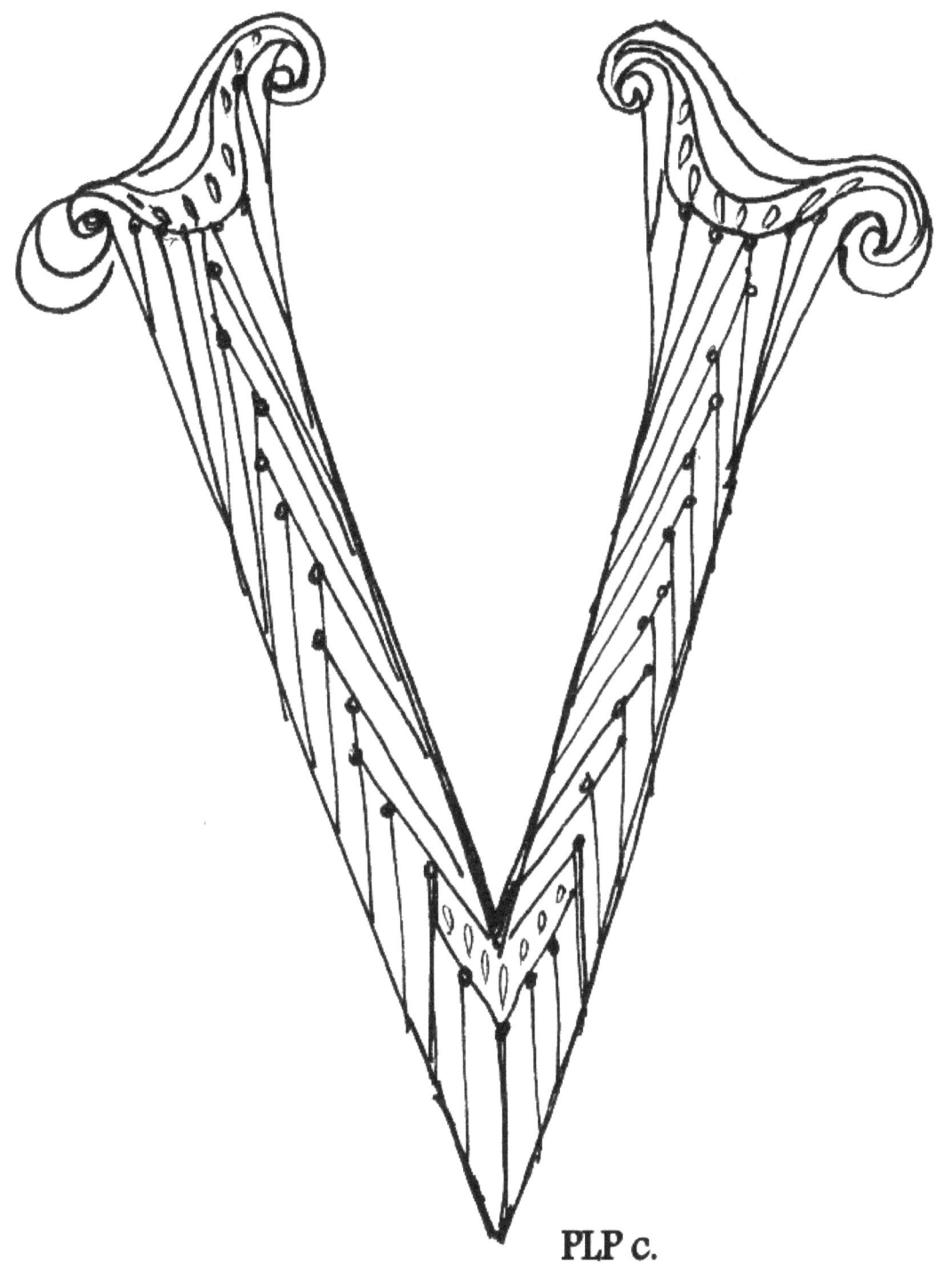

PLP c.

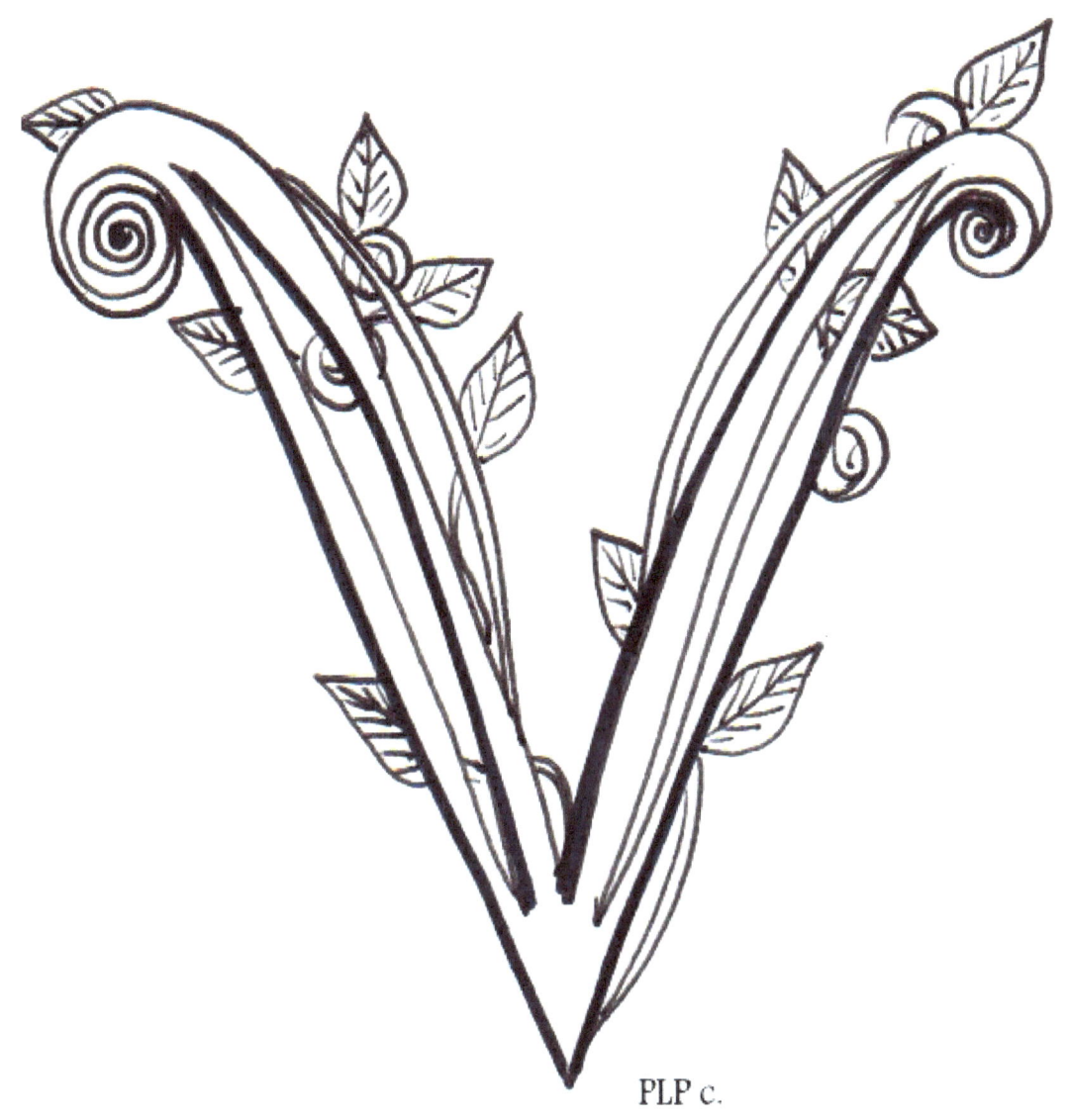

PLP c.

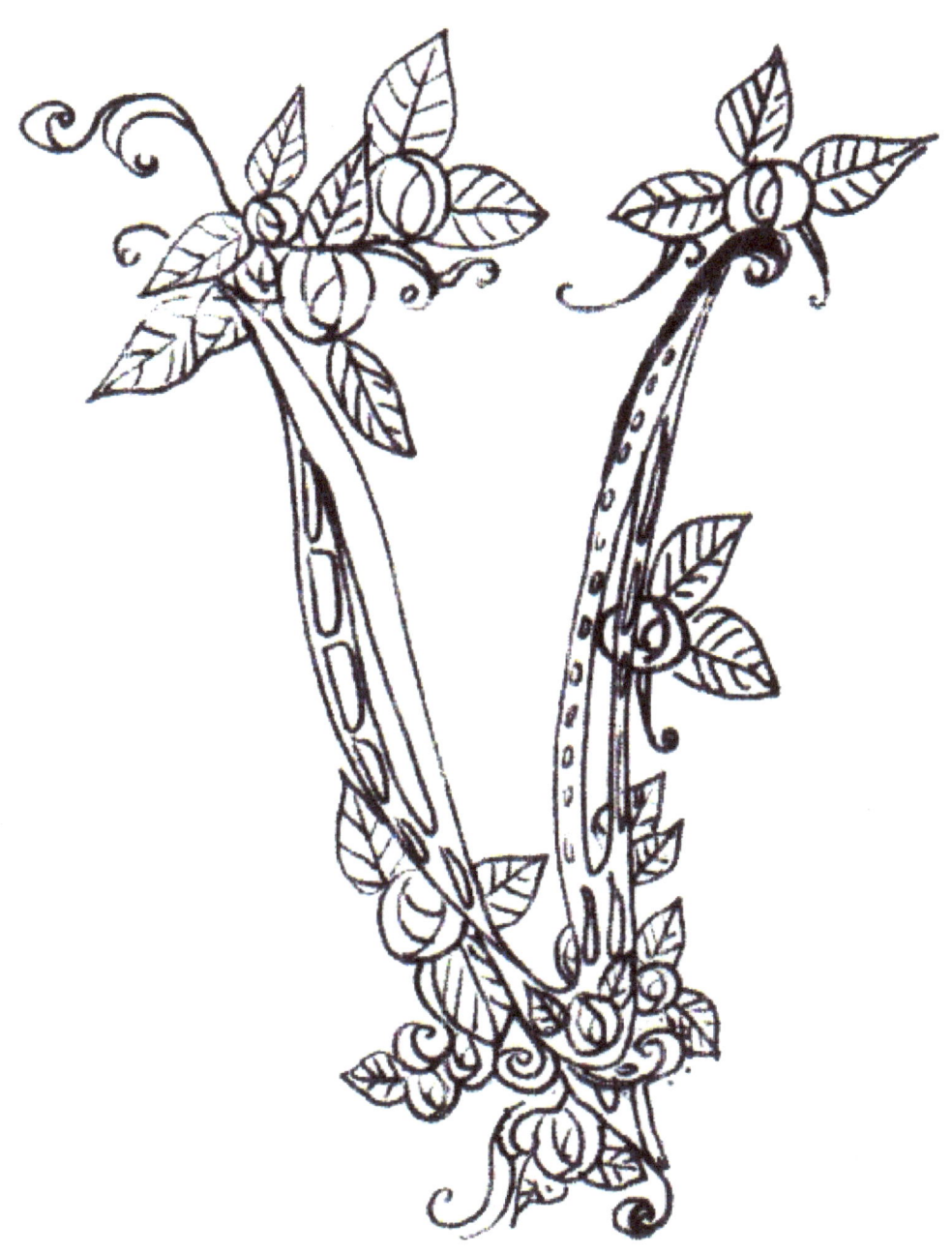

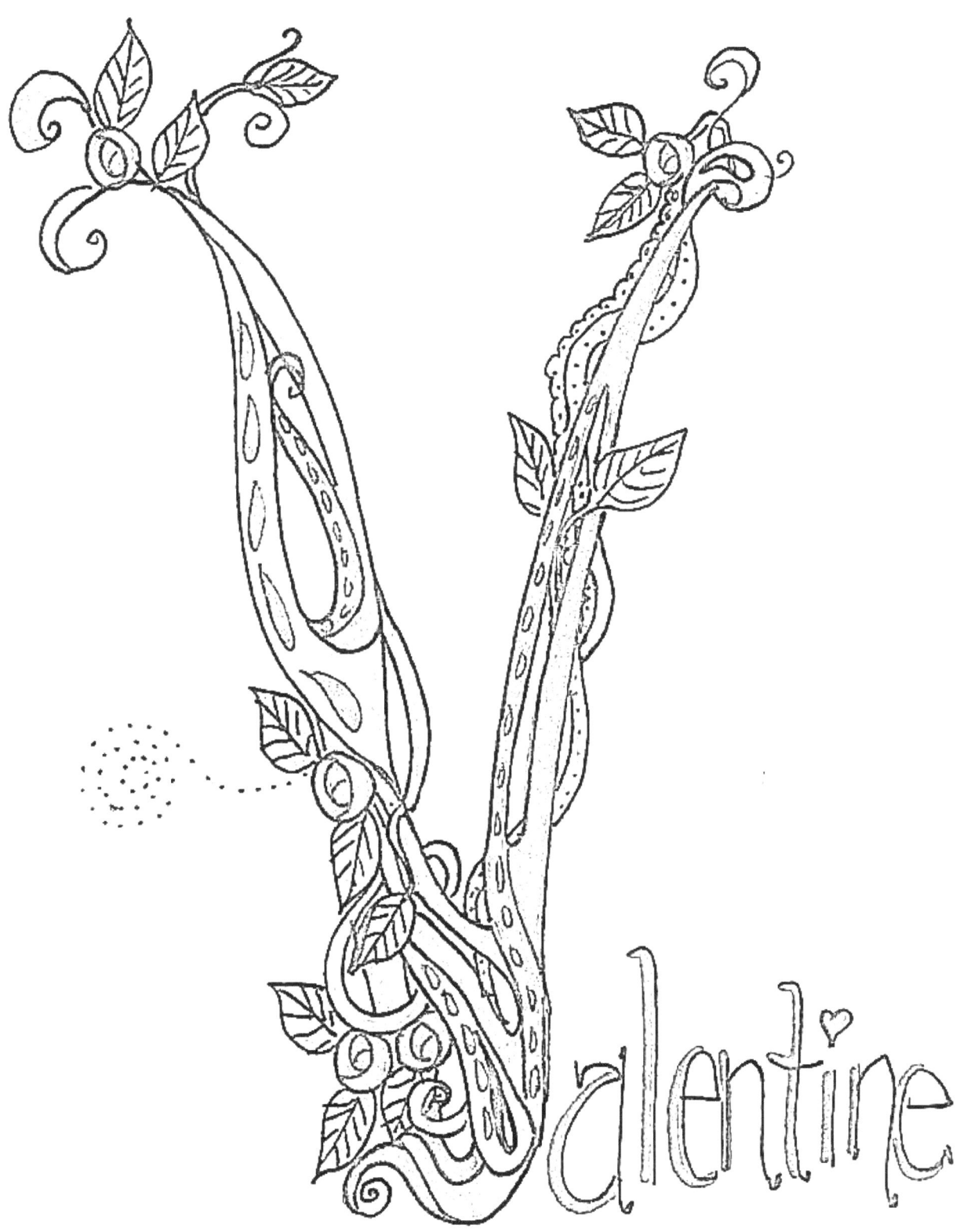

Valentine

PLP c

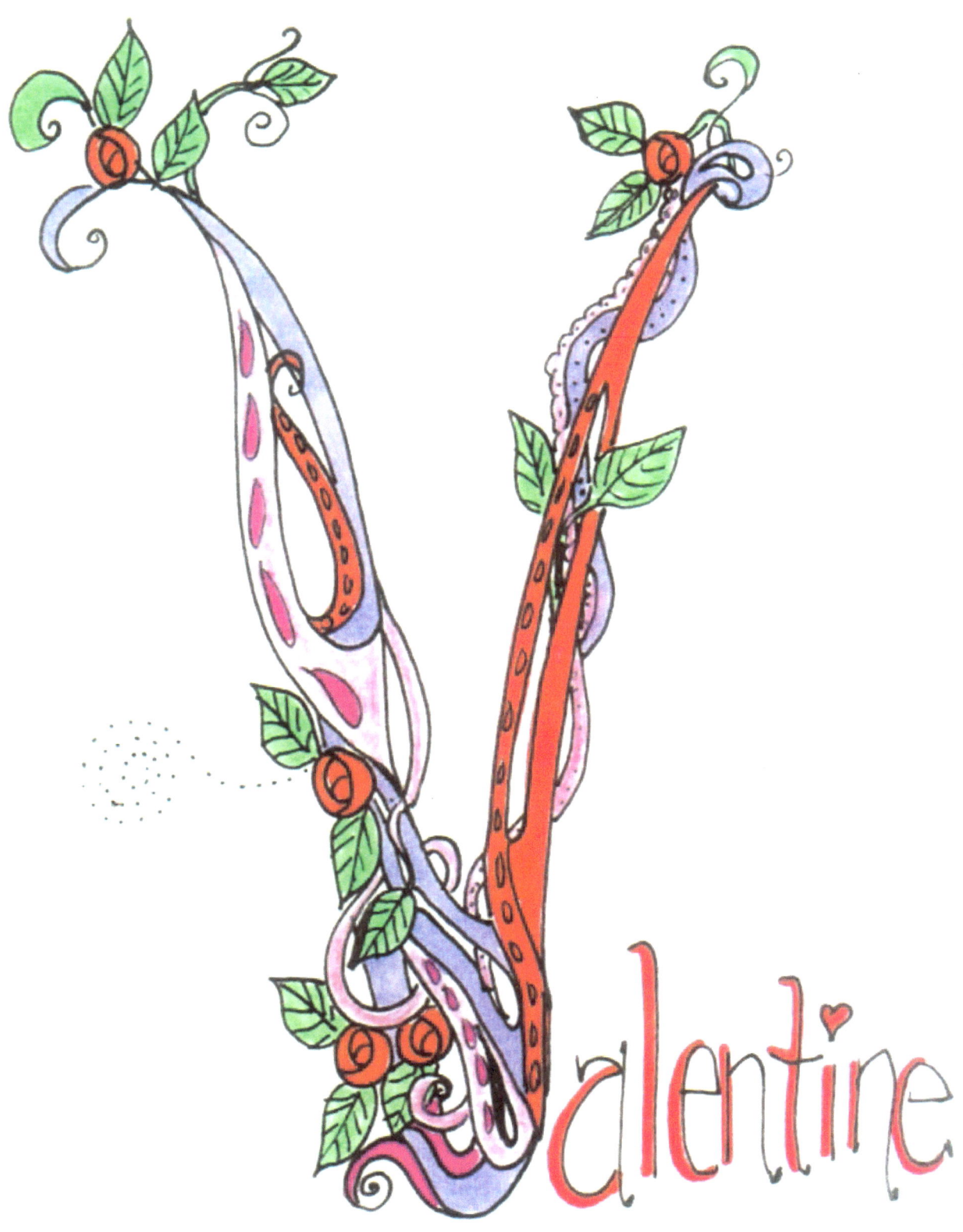

alentine

PLP c.

53

Hopefully you have enjoyed the many Victorious V letters in this book. The other letters of the alphabet each have their own book available if you are interested. These Wonder Letters have growing possibilities of color . See what you can come up with.

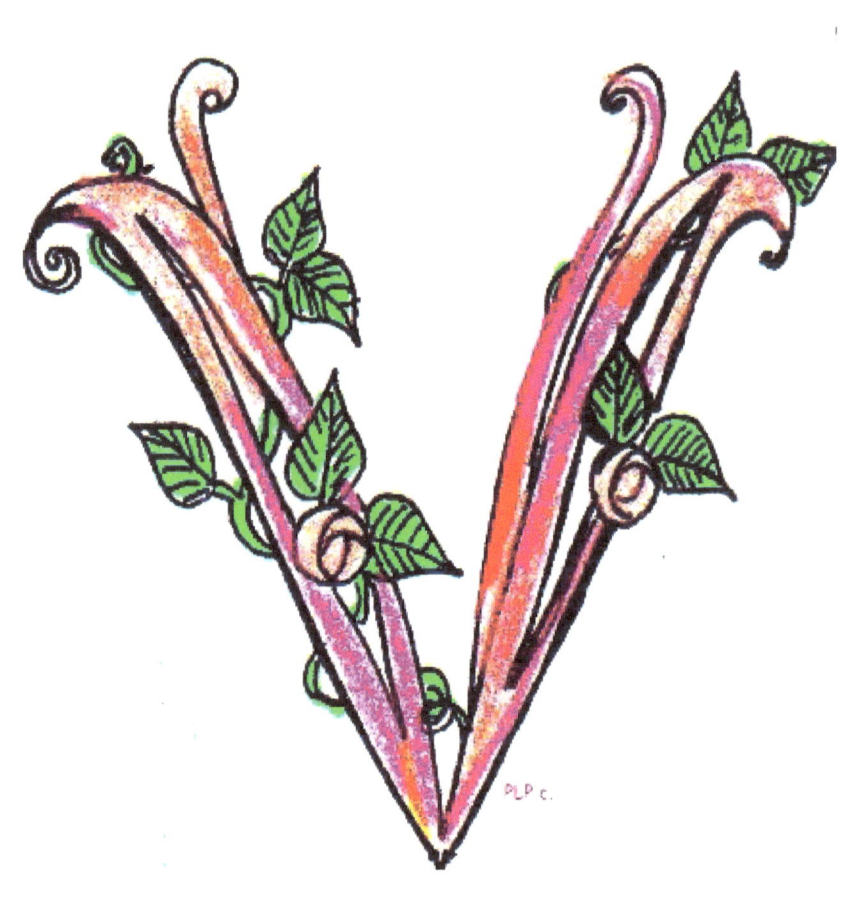

V can surely have other flowers surrounding it or no flowers. V can be an adventure to draw or color. Here is just a little V to thank you for your VISIT. After all it starts wonderful words like Valour, Victory. Valentine and Vivacious.

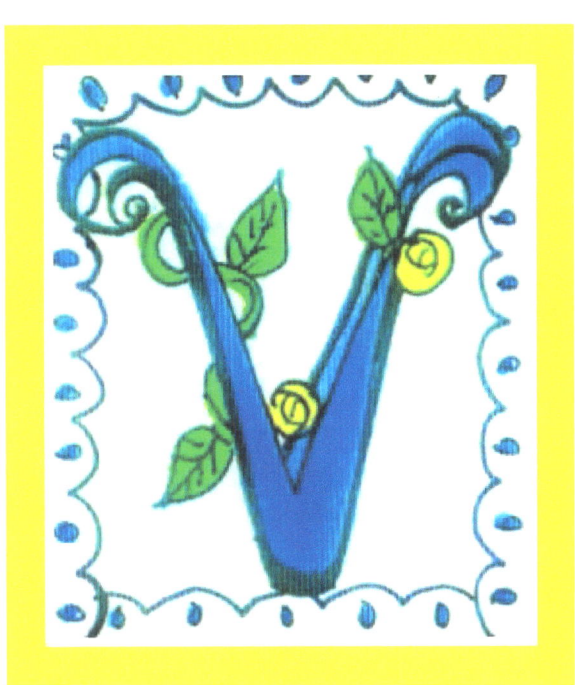